Writing Doctoral Project Proposals:

Higher Education Research

(2014)

Prof Paul Trowler

About this book

This book is designed to be as helpful as possible for anyone who needs to write a doctoral research proposal in the area of higher education research. It is concise, while still being comprehensive and useful. Its audience is prospective doctoral students who have to write a project proposal which will be assessed for admission and perhaps for a scholarship to do their doctoral research, as well as those who have already been admitted to university but now need to have a full proposal approved.

For readability, terms which may need a fuller explanation are linked from the text to a glossary at the end of the book. Terms in the text that are described in the glossary are printed in bold.

Paul Trowler is uniquely qualified to write on this topic. He is Professor of Higher Education at Lancaster University, UK. For many years he was responsible for postgraduate research student admissions to the Department of Educational Research, for organizing selection processes for doctoral scholarships and for assessing project proposals on the Doctoral Programme in Higher Education there. He has BA, MA, Cert. Ed. and PhD degrees and is an elected Fellow of the *Society for Research into Higher Education*.

All Rights Reserved © 2014 Paul Trowler

Contents

Introduction	4
Title of the Project	6
Research Questions	8
Background to the Research Topic	13
Research Design & Methods	15
Significance of the Research	30
Research Timetable	32
Writing a Bibliography	35
Finding Inspiration	36
From Sketchy Idea to Robust Project Proposal	38
Glossary	40
References	43

Introduction

Applicants for a doctoral degree and those already on a doctoral programme normally have to supply a project proposal as part of their application. For initial applicants this is one of the three ways in which universities normally make selection decisions. These three ways involve asking and answering these questions:
1. Is the applicant sufficiently qualified and capable to do a doctorate (as judged by their CV and track record)?

2. Is the research project proposal of high enough quality, practicable and important enough to be acceptable (as judged by the written proposal and perhaps a defence of it in interview)?

3. Is there a supervisor who is able and willing to supervise the proposal?

Each university's requirements regarding the research project proposal (point 2) are slightly different, but for the Department of Educational Research at Lancaster University the requirement is a fairly standard one: doctoral project proposals should be up to 1,000 words and should cover the following areas:

Title of the Research: A meaningful, provisional title that summarises the area of interest and planned programme of research. There should be a central problematic in the title, not simply a description of the field to be studied.

Research Questions: Identification of the main research question(s) being asked. These should be succinct, researchable and significant. Bullet points are usually best.

Background to the Research Topic: Explanation of how the questions are different from those asked by others, drawing on a brief review of the relevant research literature. This should show familiarity with the main literature in the field of interest.

Research Design & Methods: The 'who', 'what', 'where' and 'why' of the research plan. There should be an explanation of how the method(s) used will answer the research questions.

Significance of the Research: The contribution that this research will make. Identify the implications of the research for existing educational theories, policy or practice in higher education.

Research Timetable: A detailed timetable that shows how the research design can be managed within a three year time period (or a 5 year period for part time students).

Bibliography: The main written sources on which the research will be based.

The rest of this short book is organized with this structure at its core. At the end of the book are two chapters outlining the more creative aspects of the process of deciding on a topic and developing a proposal.

Title of the Project

The title of the proposed project is important because it sums up the focus and significance of the envisaged research. A good title should make it clear what the central problematic is, the key issue being addressed. This should be done succinctly and perhaps might even indicate the research design being used.

However many authors of doctoral proposals fail to do this and instead make one of the following three mistakes:

* Using verbs like 'explore' or 'investigate': these are too open-ended. For example: *"Exploring Teleconferencing in Further Education in the UK"*. This indicates vagueness in the mind of the candidate and the potential danger of an endless doctorate, because there are no parameters or clear goals.

* Contrasting two possibilities and asking which is correct. For example *"Positive Change or 'Self-Righteous Waffle': Academics' Perspectives on Sustainability Policy in Universities."* This indicates simplistic binary thinking and suggests that 'straw men' are being set up to be easily knocked down

* Writing a sentence which is just descriptive and lacks a problematic. For example *"The Motivational Effect of Technical and Vocational Education on Students in India."* There is no issue evident: it is unclear what the project is specifically about.

Much better are titles which give an immediate feel for the key issue at hand, and even an indication of the research design:

"Can Students Influence Policy Implementation in Higher Education? : A Case Study Based on the Mainstreaming of Liberal Adult Education." (The title of a PhD by D.F.M. Butt, Reading University, 2000).

"A critical review of the role of the English funding body for higher education in the relationship between the State and higher education in the period 1945-2003". (The title of a PhD by D.J. Taggart, Bristol University, 2004).

Research Questions

Research questions should:
- Be answerable: it must be possible to know when a question has been answered

- Be specific, that is set clear boundaries in terms of what is being studied, and what is not

- Include at least one analytical question which goes beyond the descriptive

- Be capable of **operationalisation**; that is, use concepts that can be turned into measureable, observable, describable phenomena

- Be bounded in what they require, that is they can be realistically answered given the resources available

- Be significant; that is, they should provide an answer to the '**so what**?' question - the issue of offering wider interest to a larger audience

One role of research questions is to guide research design, and there needs to be congruence between that design and the questions. This means that the research design chosen must be capable of answering the research questions.

Here is a problematic attempt at constructing research questions:

> *This project aims to explore academic staff's reception of the teaching and learning policy of a university. The analysis will focus on the discourse that arises from staff's reaction to the policy as well as factors that could undermine or facilitate the achievement of the policy.*

This is more like part of an abstract than research questions: while these statements give a feel for the proposed research, there is no specificity, only broad aims. While they give licence to the writer to cover ground that seems interesting, they fail to set boundaries. It will be unclear to the writer when their work has stepped outside the limits of the study. The word 'explore' is particularly dangerous in this respect - it does not set boundaries or specific goals. 'Reception' is capable of multiple interpretations and needs to be operationalised. There are too many questions wrapped up in these two sentences: they need to be unpicked.

Those two sentences could be reconfigured as follows:

1. To what extent do academic staff in one Faculty in a new university in the UK display knowledge about and understanding of the formal teaching and learning policy there?

2. In what different ways do academic staff there interpret and respond to that policy?

3. What reasons can be given for the differences identified in answering questions 1 and 2?

4. What different **discursive repertoires** do they draw on when they discuss the policy?

5. What are the implications of the answers to questions 1-4 for policy implementation in the area of teaching and learning in the case study university?

6. To what extent do these findings confirm what is known about policy implementation in that context?

7. What are the implications of the findings for university managers at senior and middle levels in that context?

These research questions, unpicked in this way, themselves raise issues about the **truth claims** that can be made from a study of one Faculty in one university, but recognising this as an issue is enough for a project proposal.

Analysing these questions further:

Question 1 requires a fairly descriptive answer but there are more analytical ones to follow.

Question 2 is possibly still too open, but it is an improvement on the original version.

Question 3 allows the writer to do some analysis which might get him or her into disciplinary differences, institutional location etc. The data collection needs to be thoughtfully constructed to be able to answer it, and a pilot study undertaken to ensure this.

Question 4 (based on the original version) stands out as possibly belonging to a different thesis, and being potentially too big, especially when Question 5 is attempted.

Question 6 allows a discussion of the literature and gives the thesis a theoretical edge.

Question 7 might be further refined, or possibly dropped if the thesis becomes too big - question 6 covers some of this already. It also begs the **'so what'** question – why should anyone other than senior and middle managers in that institution be interested?

Because of question 6 the main answer to the 'so what' question appears to be a theoretical one in relation to the literature on policy implementation. That would be fine, and the applicant needs to make it clear that this is the main priority of the project, with other aims being significant but perhaps not central.

Often it is useful to distinguish between the **locus** and the **focus** of a doctoral proposal – a topic of study can be merely the location through which deeper questions are explored. In this case the locus is the teaching and learning policy in one Faculty in one university, but the focus is actually achieving a better understanding of the implementation of change. Research question 6 is the key one, if this approach were to be taken in this example.

Research Questions: The seven deadly sins

1. Too descriptive – *"What are the management styles in place in Saudi Arabian universities?"* (This is OK if there are more analytical questions after it, though of course it is ambitious).

2. Too narrow – *"How can the use of e-portfolios at the University of Bentham be improved?"* (Who cares – apart from people at Bentham?).

3. Too ambitious – *"What teaching and learning approaches are in place in UK higher education and how can they be improved?"* (Impossible to answer).

4. Only focused on perceptions – *"In what different ways do Accountancy lecturers at the University of Bentham view the merger of their Department with the Department of Statistics there?"* (**So what**?).

5. Too vague – *"How does the higher education system in Chile differ from that in Argentina"?* (How long have you got?).

6. **Normative** – *"What are the benefits of linking research and teaching in universities?"* (What about the dysfunctions?).

7. Too **prescriptive** – *"Why does the modular system in UK higher education need to be changed?"* (Predicts the outcome without actually doing the research).

Note how the deadly sins are rarely found alone – problematic questions often combine two or more.

Background to the Research Topic

The background section of a research project proposal should set out the background to the issue for research: this will definitely include the relevant literature but (depending on the topic) might also include the policy background, the contemporary relevance of the topic or some other background factors that are relevant.

The aim of this section is to demonstrate a reasonable knowledge of the area (recognising of course that the research hasn't been done yet), to situate the issue for the panel assessing the application, to show why the proposed research is important, and to show what the research could offer that is significant.

The section should not be too long: often candidates assume that a very extended discussion of the literature will impress. Of course to some extent it does, especially when that discussion shows the ability to evaluate research critically. However, more impressive is the thinking behind the description of the proposed research itself when this demonstrates clarity in conceptualising a very concrete, doable and clearly envisaged research design, the outcomes of which will advance knowledge in some way. So the background section needs to be kept fairly brief, and the discussion of the literature oriented to showing where there are deficiencies or gaps that will be addressed by the research.

It is important not to simply take descriptive content straight from websites or other sources. Apart from the potential issue of plagiarism, that content is unlikely to oriented to the proposed topic of research. It is really important that all aspects of the background section are situated in relation to the specifics of the proposed research. Too often in doctoral proposals descriptive material is dissociated from any attempt to demonstrate its significance.

Research Design & Methods

This is probably the hardest part of writing a research proposal, and is often very significant in terms of whether the whole proposal is convincing or not. Clearly, once enrolled, the candidate's supervisor will help him or her to develop a good research design. But it is necessary to make a convincing attempt at it in the research proposal.

Sometimes candidates fall back on **grounded theory** in developing their proposals: basically arguing that they will collect the data and see what comes out of them. However this often fails to convince selection panels and in general it is better to set out a clear, convincing, planned research design. The key thing in this is to make sure that the design chosen is capable of answering the research questions; indeed is the *best* way to answer the research questions.

In general the research design should make clear:

- what the units of analysis are (institutions, departments, people);

- which (or which types of these) of these will be selected for data collection, how many and why;

- what type of data collection methods will be used, and why;

- how the data will be analysed.

Often, a diagram can sum up the descriptive elements of the above more clearly and succinctly than can a written description. But of course the rationale for the design needs to be elaborated in writing.

Ethical issues need to be addressed, as do questions of access: it is often harder to secure agreement to participate than is at first imagined, even for insider researchers: simply assuming that the data will be easily obtainable is not convincing, but thinking ahead about this at least demonstrates awareness of the issue.

Questions and answers

The key issue in research design is ensuring that the decisions made are guided by the research questions: the data generated by the research must be appropriate and sufficient to provide robust answers to the questions asked. It is also important to ensure that a consistent and defensible approach is taken towards **epistemological** and **ontological** issues: what does the research claim can be known about the social reality under investigation and how is that reality conceived?

A **realist** ontological position will usually mean more positivist research designs utilising predominantly quantitative data generation approaches which yield statements describing correlations of a generalisable nature. On the other hand a social constructionist position is likely to be more qualitatively inclined and quite limited in its claims for generalisability.

There are many excellent textbooks on research design, data collection and the role of theory. Here I concentrate on the key issues of relevance to insider researchers.

The following section on research design and methods is drawn from my book on **Insider Research in Universities**, aimed at those researching or planning to research the institution in which they are employed or are currently a student. For more information on this area, including 'outsider' research, see the latest edition of Judith Bell's book *Doing Your Research Project*.

Single and multi-site studies

Insider researchers are usually faced with multiple pressures on their time and limited resources to use in the research. Some will be employed by the university and have more financial resources but limited time for the research, others will be full-time students studying their own university, with more time but less cash. In either case the option of doing a single-site case study is attractive for practical reasons, and as the next chapter shows can be valuable in itself. Coleman and von Hellermann (eds, 2011) and their contributors advocate doing ethnographic studies based on anthropological methods conducted on the researcher's own 'turf':

> ...the 'field' has traditionally been conceptualized as being 'out there' (away from the anthropologist's home), enclosed within a definable territory, and best understood through the method of participant observation. Bound up with these practices is the assumption that culture is located 'out there', with ethnography being about the unfamiliar 'other'. Participant observation traditionally involves intensive dwelling and interaction with the 'native' in order to understand his or her worldview...Such positing of people, places, and 'culture' is increasingly critiqued on account of the problematic ideological assumptions..." (Mand, 2011: 42)

These assumptions include the notion that 'culture' is something exotic and 'other', amenable only to the distanced and more analytical academic eye, eventually represented through the godlike authorial voice. Insider research which views the local and familiar is at least as valuable, they argue. But as well as seeing the value of single-site insider research, Coleman and von Hellerman explore the problems and possibilities of *multi*-site ethnographies including those conducted 'at home'. However, as Marcus acknowledges (p. 27, in Coleman and von Hellerman), attempting to deploy such a labour-intensive method of data collection as ethnography in multiple sites will "overwhelm the norms of intensive, patient work in ethnography".

For the individual researcher such a design is too ambitious. This means that a multi-site approach which uses mixed methods or less labour-intensive methods than ethnography may have benefits which justify their costs in terms of time and labour. The important issue in making decisions around this is appropriateness in terms of the research questions, which themselves then come into the mix of factors to consider when planning research which is both practicable and valuable.

For the insider researcher developing a project which compares results from their own institution to those elsewhere, a multi-site study is obviously the way to go - unless other studies have already been conducted elsewhere which are close enough to their own.

Examples of such comparative projects include:

1. The factors influencing the success or otherwise of an innovation

2. Approaches to management and leadership and their effectiveness

3. The implementation of a national policy at ground level, including compliance (or otherwise) with national quality (or other) guidelines

4. Professional practices in a discipline or field of study

5. Student responses to an innovation

Action research

Bensimon et al (2004: 105) suggest that it is important for practitioners concerned with bringing about change in their context to "produce knowledge in local contexts to identify problems and take action to solve them". The authors in that collection advocate the idea that change agents should be 'practitioners-as-researchers'.

Action research is an emergent enquiry process involving cycles of: actions; enquiry, analysis; planning; changed actions. It has, broadly, an enhancement agenda. But there are ofen different understandings of what 'enhancement' may involve, especially among those on the ground in universities.

Action research can be undertaken with different audiences, beneficiaries and purposes in mind. It can be emancipatory in intent, aiming to identify disadvantaged groups and to rectify structural disadvantage, or it can simply be aimed at making sure policy is implemented effectively, regardless of what it is or its effects.

Useful guides to conducting action research are Coghlan and Brannick (2010) and Koshy (2009).

Evaluative research

Evaluative research in higher education aims to attribute value and worth to individual, group, institutional or sectoral activities happening there (Saunders, Trowler and Bamber, 2011). Because this guide concentrates on insider research, the relevant levels of evaluative activity are the individual, group and university ones. Such research asks questions about the value of long-standing activities or of innovations that the researcher is undertaking, or those of a group to which s/he belongs, or those of the university as a whole.

While evaluative research often deploys similar data generation techniques to those of 'regular' research, and can use theory in similar ways too, there is one key question presented by this kind of research if it is to be lifted beyond the particular. That is – 'what is the value of this in terms of a larger contribution to knowledge in the academic world?' If the research focuses on the value of a particular set of activities, or an innovation, in a particular location at a particular time, then it becomes difficult to answer that question. Furthermore, the chances of getting a study of a particular situation published in a reputable journal are rather small, if that is an aim of the research.

There are three key ways in which evaluative studies can be conducted so that they provide good answers to this 'contribution' question and stand a good chance of being published, at least in part. These are: *theoretical* contribution; *methodological* contribution; *professional* contribution. Often good evaluative studies will offer a combination of these.

The *theoretical* contribution relates to some aspect of the relevant literature, perhaps on implementation theory or the management of change, or some aspect of theory related to the substance of the activity or innovation (information and communication technologies, for example). The later part of this chapter deals with the place of theory in research.

The *methodological* contribution relates to evaluative methodology, the techniques and theories employed in conducting evaluative research, and the study should offer something additional to what already exists in this area. There are a number of different approaches to evaluative research, methodologically and in other ways, so the contribution can be made to one or more of these. In summary they are: technical-rational evaluation; appreciative enquiry (**Cooperrider and Srivastva**, 1987); utilization-focused evaluation (Patton, 1997) and finally realistic evaluation (Pawson and Tilley, 1997). An overview of these is offered in chapter 2 of Saunders, Trowler and Bamber, 2011.

Finally, the *professional* contribution relates to practice in the area being investigated, and to achieve this it is necessary to expand the truth claims of the research beyond simply establishing the value of the particular activity or innovation to encompass *similar* activities/innovations in similar circumstances. In this third category the issues covered in the next chapter become particularly relevant.

Institutional ethnography

This is an approach to researching what its founder, Dorothy Smith (2005; 2006), describes as the "textually-mediated social organization". Smith says that institutional ethnography begins by locating a standpoint within an institutional order, a particular guiding perspective from which to explore that order.

This raises a set of concerns, issues or problem germane to those people who occupy that standpoint. These "local actualities of the everyday world" (Smith, 2005: 34) are only the starting point however. From here the investigation of institutional processes is launched, and the broader structural forces which impinge on the everyday world are explored. Because of this unfolding from the local it is not always possible to sketch a detailed research design in advance. But Smith argues that the design is not random: "Each next step builds from what has been discovered and invades more extended dimensions of the institutional regime" (2005: 35). Language, and textual objects are very significant in this – for Smith language serves to co-ordinate subjectivities.

Devault (2006: 294) says this:

> Institutional ethnographies are built from the examination of work processes and study of how they are coordinated, typically through texts and discourses of various sorts. Work activities are taken as the fundamental grounding of social life, and an institutional ethnography generally takes some particular experience (and associated work processes) as a "point of entry." The work involved could be part of a paid job; it might fall into the broader field of unpaid or invisible work, as so much of women's work does; or it might comprise the activities of some "client" group.

This examination is conducted through the standard mix of ethnographic approaches; interviews, observation, documentary analysis and so on. But careful attention is paid in particular to the use of textual artefacts, the discursive repertoires employed in them and the causes of effects of these on social relations within organizations.

In Smith's original formulation there is a concern to investigate the ruling relations that are articulated in work processes and instantiated in texts, and she pays particular attention to the ways in which women are subjugated within institutional processes and through texts and discourses. For example in universities 'mothering work' can be a discursively and organizationally embedded in such a way that women academics disproportionately find themselves doing low-status and unrecognised work supporting students in difficulties. And of course what in some contexts are called 'support staff' are disproportionately female in most universities.

How this has come to be, and how it is perpetuated, are areas that can usefully be explored in a fine-grained way through institutional ethnography. And not only explored. A key tenet of the approach is that it should be *for* people and not just *about* them: the research must illuminate the mechanisms of oppression and disadvantage and suggest ameliorative strategies.

Institutional ethnography sees local practices in terms of the larger picture of structured advantage and disadvantage, despite the fact that it starts from a particular standpoint within the institution. In this it addresses one of the criticisms sometimes made of fine-grained ethnographic research, for example by Hamersley (1993) and Porter (1993), that such research loses sight of the structural constraints on actors and structural conditioning of their behaviour.

It is clear that insider research and institutional ethnography are highly compatible, at least for some kinds of research questions. However as an approach to enquiry it does leave the researcher with some problematic questions. One is: what standpoint should I start from and how do I draw the limits around it? This is a question of level of analysis: the standpoint might be that of 'students', or 'women students', or 'women students with disabilities'. That last category could itself be segmented further. Another question is: if I start from one standpoint and work outwards, as Smith recommends, what about other standpoints that exist in the university – why should I privilege just this one? These and many other questions need good answers if readers are to be convinced that the study is robust.

Hypothesis testing

Here the purpose of insider research is to test an hypothesis or to replicate a previous study in a different but relevant context in order to test its conclusions. Either qualitative or quantitative approaches may be adopted to do this, or a combination of both.

This research purpose is best illustrated by an example. Such research could involve a study designed to test the hypothesis developed by Arum and Roksa (2011) that universities (at least in the USA) are "academically adrift". Arum and Roksa used the Collegiate Learning Assessment, a standardized test administered to students in their first semester and then again at the end of their second year, as well as survey responses to answer the question: "do students learn the important things that universities claim to deliver?" They conclude that 45 percent of the students included in their data demonstrate no significant improvement in critical thinking, complex reasoning, and writing during their first two years of college.

In addition Arum and Roksa extrapolate from their analysis some explanations: one is that students are distracted from their studies by socializing or by working at the same time. A further cause is the fact that universities and their staff prioritise other things than undergraduate learning, such as research. In addition there is, they claim, deliberate collusion between staff and students not to tax each other too much.

Methodologically this study has come under criticism, most notably from Alexander **Astin** (2011), and there are many claims in it that are unsubstantiated and which from a UK perspective appear to be just wrong (for example about the findings of the majority of studies on the 'teaching-research nexus').

So, this study could be tested in a different but relevant context. A similar or identical research design could be adopted to test the findings, and the same statistical techniques could be applied to the data. Alternatively the hypothesised causes of this claimed lack of significant learning could be explored. A further alternative is to build on Astin's critique and design a 'better' study.

Theory and insider research

Theory-use is very important in research generally and insider research in particular – it lifts it above mere market research or journalism, and it allows the researcher to step outside generally accepted ways of seeing the social world.

'Theory' is usually portrayed as consisting of six linked characteristics:

> 1. It uses a set of interconnected concepts to classify the components of a system and how they are related.
>
> 2. This set is deployed to develop a set of systematically and logically related propositions that depict some aspect of the operation of the world.

3. These claim to provide an explanation for a range of phenomena by illuminating causal connections.

4. Theory should provide predictions which reduce uncertainty about the outcome of a specific set of conditions. These may be rough probabilistic or fuzzy predictions, and they should be corrigible – it should be possible to disconfirm or jeopardize them through observations of the world. In the **hypothetico-deductive** tradition, from which this viewpoint comes, theory offers statements of the form 'in Z conditions, if X happens then Y will follow'.

5. Theory helps locate local social processes in wider structures, because it is these which lend predictability to the social world.

6. Finally, theory guides research interventions, helping to define research problems and appropriate research designs to investigate them.

Different levels and types of theory inform decisions, processes and outcomes in research (see Trowler, 2012, for an account of them).

There are also different views on the role of theory, some challenging its fundamental role, as set out above, and seeing it not as part of a 'scientific' process but as creative and emancipatory. Feminist thinkers, among others, tend to adopt this perspective:

> how often their own cherished analytical rationality is broken up by glimpses into the imagination of more provocative thinkers. I have come to the conclusion that it is not so much that we self-consciously assemble all the resources for the making of research imaginaries as those vivid ideas (and frequently their authors) come to haunt us. (Hey, 2006: 439)

Stephen Ball agrees:

> Theory is a vehicle for 'thinking otherwise', it is a platform for 'outrageous hypotheses' and for 'unleashing criticism'. Theory

is destructive, disruptive and violent. It offers a language for challenge, and modes of thought, other than those articulated for us by dominant others. It provides a language of rigour and irony rather than contingency. The purpose of such theory is to de-familiarise present practices and categories, to make them seem less self-evident and necessary, and to open up spaces for the invention of new forms of experience. (Ball, 1995: 265-6)

Haraway (1991) takes this point further in elaborating the notion of 'standpoint theory'. Sprague and Hayes, 2000, in discussing the concept, say this:

Standpoint epistemology argues that all knowledge is constructed in a specific matrix of physical location, history, culture, and interests... A standpoint is not the spontaneous thinking of a person or a category of people. Rather, it is the combination of resources available in a specific context from which an understanding might be constructed. (Sprague and Hayes, 2000: 673).

For Sprague and Hayes, as for Smith (2005), discussed above, it is important to challenge the standpoint of the privileged from the standpoint of the disadvantaged and (as feminists) from that of women. This can bring empowerment and self-determination; it uses theory as a weapon against structures of privilege and structured disadvantage.

Feminist standpoint theory suggests that an important way to develop this line of research is to build on the standpoints of those who are least empowered in our current relationships. People living in different intersections of gender, class, and race are likely to have different stories to tell. Thus, a good way to start is to listen to people with disabilities who are also women and/or poor and/or people of color, and the people who nurture them, as they describe in their own ways the constraints on their daily lives... (Sprague and Hayes, 2000: 690).

Insider research presents particular problems in terms of the use of theory and the relationship between theory and data. Insiders conducting emic research are themselves liable to be influenced by tacit theories held by respondents, or even they can even be captured by institutional or by management discourse, as Hammersley argues (see Trowler, 2001, for more on this).

In such cases it becomes particularly difficult to render the normal strange, to move beyond the standpoint of the privileged. But human behaviour viewed through the microscope tends to bring to attention impalpable drivers far more than when it is seen through a telescope and by their nature these are difficult to apprehend through pure empiricism. In fine-grained qualitative insider research knowledgeability and sense-making are foregrounded as explanation is prioritised above simple correlation. In this respect the role of theory in insider research holds both promise and dangers.

Research Design and Methods: The seven deadly sins

1. Not being specific enough about the details of the sample selected for study and the rationale for that selection.
2. Adopting a research design which is not appropriate to answering the research questions.
3. Not giving a rationale for the overall research design.
4. Proposing a 'convenience' sampling approach without acknowledging the consequences of this for the robustness of the study: being too complacent about what is acceptable.
5. Not explaining how the different components of the research design can be integrated during analysis – especially in a mixed-methods design.
6. Not acknowledging potential ethical issues.
7. Not giving a convincing answer to the '**so what**' question in terms of what the data can offer.

Significance of the Research

Doctoral research must demonstrate that a significant contribution has been made to knowledge in its field, and must at least in part be publishable in an academic journal.

While it might be presumptuous to identify so far in advance what that significant contribution will be, it is important to show that the research at least has the potential to jump this hurdle. Doubts about this might be raised in admission panel members' minds if the topic of the research appears to be too parochial; only concerned with the issues in one organization at a particular time, for example. These concerns may be magnified if the research design involves insider research. I deal with this in more detail in Chapter 4, *Value and Robustness*, of **Doing Insider Research in Universities**.

So in making it explicit why the research is important, and at a high enough level potentially to merit a doctorate, it is important to go beyond the particular. In discussing evaluative research in the previous chapter I identified some potential avenues for doing this. For other kinds of research alternative ways in which this can be done include:

- Testing, developing or elaborating a particular theoretical perspective or tradition

- Testing previous research findings in a new context

- Approaching questions previously addressed by other research using new methodological tools

- Developing conceptual models which illuminate some aspect of social reality

- Critiquing current positions in literature, policy or practice

- Building a basis for new policy or practice in wider contexts

- Developing new approaches to research

- Offering new insights into significant issues

- Bringing together and building on previous research findings

Research Timetable

The key point in setting out the research timetable is to be realistic. An over-ambitious timetable betrays lack of insight into the research process.

Time should be allocated at the beginning of the research for in-depth familiarisation with the literature and for refining the research design and questions as well as for developing data collection instruments. This almost always takes longer than expected: getting to grips with the literature will need to incorporate literature on relevant theory, on the substantive topic and on research methodology, so this alone is time-consuming.

It is important to conduct a pilot study (assuming the proposed research is empirically-based) before going into the field. Time needs to be allocated to this, and to processing the results from that pilot.

The time allocated to data collection and analysis depends, of course, on the research design, but again needs to be realistic. In most cases data analysis will occur concurrently with data generation rather than being a process left undone until after all the data have been 'collected'.

Writing up the thesis also takes longer than is sometimes imagined. A typical thesis will have six or seven chapters, and even with drafts of many of these already prepared, it can take between three and eight months of dedicated work to refine the whole thesis into a finished form. Setting out the structure of the thesis here can be helpful, serving to emphasise the clarity of the proposal. A fairly standard set of chapters looks like this:

1. Introduction

2. Contextualisation

3. Literature review

4. Method/ology

5. Data presentation and analysis

6. Conclusions

Different universities set different targets for their doctoral students, but the **Department of Educational Research** at Lancaster University sets the ones below. Such targets can act as a template for setting out the research timetable in a doctoral project proposal:

For Students in Year 1 (or Part-Time Equivalent):
- Research questions and research design finalised and agreed with supervisor.

- Good progress made with review of relevant literature.

- Scoping and pilot enquiries have validated research design in terms of potential of richness of data to answer questions.

- Key concepts and theoretical lens clear by end of year 1.

For Students in Year 2 (or Part-Time Equivalent):
- Data collection complete, or nearly so. Good progress on analysis.

- Some thesis chapters written in draft, including contextual-introductory chapters, methodology chapter, literature review.

- Good conceptualisation of probable findings and argument, including its engagement with the literature.

- Writing 'voice' for thesis now found.

For Students in Year 3 (or Part-Time Equivalent):
- Data analysis complete. Argument fully formed.

- Writing up full thesis.

- Presentations at conferences and departmental seminar to prepare for viva and improve structure of argument.

- Potential areas of discussion in viva identified and prepared for.

Writing a Bibliography

The key things in setting out the bibliography are: a) to set out in full the bibliographical details of any works cited in the proposal and b) to indicate other significant texts that will inform the project.

In doing this the panel assessing the project proposal will look for coverage of the field and for good practice in both citation and setting out a bibliography. Inconsistencies in how books and articles are referenced may be taken as a sign of poor research training or sloppiness in writing, and so should be avoided.

In research into higher education the usual citation and referencing conventions involve a version of the Harvard system. The style guide for authors from, for example, Open University press, is (in most cases) appropriate for a doctoral proposal for higher education research: **http://mcgraw-hill.co.uk/openup/authors.html**

Finding Inspiration

Often doctoral applicants and candidates have a firm view of the topic they want to research. This may be some issue that is important to them professionally, a puzzle that they want to spend time exploring great depth. It may have been suggested to them by a comment from a colleague, or by something they read. They may simply be continuing earlier studies but now within a much more focused and deeper doctoral framework. Turning this topic into a robust project proposal is the topic of the next chapter.

Sometimes though they do not have a very clear idea about what the topic of their doctoral research might be, or have two or three different ones and they are not sure which is the most viable.

In this latter case there are a number of ways of finding inspiration for researchable topics:

* Reading titles and abstracts of completed doctorates in the higher education field for areas that are of interest. Where there is access to the complete doctorate, looking for sections on 'further research' can be helpful. See ethos.bl.uk and http://www.theses.com/.

* Reflecting on what area of expertise they would like to be known for in four or five years' time, or what would be professionally most valuable.

* Reflecting on what kind of data collection methods would be most viable and interesting for them, and working back from that to a suitable topic.

* Reviewing topics currently being funded by relevant higher education research funding bodies such as (in the UK) the ESRC, HEA and LFHE.

* Investigating the website of preferred university departments to explore the research specialisms of likely supervisors.

* Reading books that give overviews of areas of research that are of interest with a view to exploring one of those areas further.
* Attending conferences and talking to people giving presentations on topics of interest about further research areas.
* Brainstorming and then progressively refining/combining ideas. See James Hayton's video on this: http://www.youtube.com/watch?v=PY01A-jCuOA&feature=player_embedded&CMP= .
(There are more resources about thesis writing from Hayton at http://3monththesis.com/)

From Sketchy Idea to Robust Project Proposal

STAGE	A Specific Example (for illustration only – a full proposal would have more)
Refine research questions	*"To what extent ,and to what ends, can conceptions of 'learning organizations' as developed in management literature be applied in university contexts in the UK?"*
Develop research design appropriate for research questions	Review of management literature on 'learning organizations'. Secondary data from a varied sample of UK universities.
If necessary revisit research questions to establish better fit with research design	*"To what extent can models of 'learning organizations' as developed in management literature be used to establish how far UK universities fit those models, using secondary data? How far do those models need development for a UK university context, and what purposes would such a development serve?"*
Identify relevant literature to be addressed	Management literature on 'learning organizations'.
Refine research design in a detailed way, especially in terms of sampling	15 UK universities will be sampled. Three will be selected from each of the 5 HE groupings in that country (Russell; Million+; 1994; University Alliance; UKADIA), with each of these further subdivided on the basis of dimensions of their strategic plans. The rationale for these decisions is based on differences in university goals, stakeholders, resources and environment, all of which will have a bearing on what it means to be a learning organization and

	how far that can be achieved.
Refine data collection and analysis methods	Content analysis of 15 university websites, followed by more detailed discourse analysis of parts of the websites of 5 of these.
Consider appropriate theoretical lens and rationale for it	Social practice theory takes the concept of the learning organization beyond idealised criteria.
Reconsider research design if necessary	Social practice theory addresses recurrent practices, values and attitudes. Therefore empirical data will be required generating detailed qualitative data.
Consider title for project	*"Reconceptualising the Concept of 'Learning Organization' for the UK Higher Education Context: Applying a social practice approach"*
Develop an account of the significance of the project in terms of original contribution to knowledge	Develops the notion of the 'learning organization' in a way which is applicable to and valuable for UK higher education. Applies the social practice lens to critique some earlier approaches to the concept of the 'learning organization' and show how it can be developed. Theoretical work has significance for the practices of universities working towards enhancing the organizational learning that occurs in those contexts.

Glossary

Academic register: A register is a particular tone and use of words that are appropriate to a given social setting. So academic register is one used in the context of writing academic books, articles or a doctorate. It is formal, tends to use Latinate words, uses compound nouns, passive voice and so on.

Action research: A cyclical process of collecting and analysing data, reflection and taking or amending action in order to bring about enhancement in practices and outcomes in the area being researched.

Advance organizer: "An advance organizer is information that is presented prior to learning and that can be used by the learner to organize and interpret new incoming information" (Mayer, 2007).

Cherry picking: In this context, being consistently selective about the data or literature used in order to substantiate an argument already formulated.

Conceptual closure: Deciding too early about the conclusions that can be derived from the data, and so ignoring evidence which contradicts those.

Discursive repertoires: Recurrently-used phrases, words, images or metaphors which situate the world in specific ways.

Elite policy study: A research project which studies top-level policy-makers or those who implement policy.

Empirical: Using primary data, collecting evidence from the world or observing it.

Empiricism: An approach to research which focuses on factual data without explicit or acknowledged use of theory, usually adopting a foundationalist position (see below).

Ethnography: A research approach which draws on multiple data sources to provide a detailed account of a cultural field.

Epistemology: Theories of knowledge and what can be known.

Foundationalism: An ontological position which holds that external reality exists independent from humans' apprehension of it.

Grounded Theory: An approach to research which begins with data collection and from that process generates a series of concepts which have explanatory power. It is an inductive approach rather than the more usual hypothetico-deductive one. The latter begins with hypotheses and theory and tests them against data using a design which arises from the logic of the hypothesis.

Hypothetico-deductive tradition: An approach to research which involves establishing an hypothesis and then testing it against reality. Part of the scientific method.

Incommensurability: A situation in which theoretical positions are adopted which take such different ontological and epistemological standpoints that they are not comparable with each other, leaving no grounds for determining which is the most accurate.

Insider research: The study of social institutions by those who are actors in them. See Trowler (2012a) for more information on doing insider research.

Instrumentalism: Ideas guided by a desire for practical application, their value being measured by the success of the outcomes of that action.

Methods: In research, includes the specific techniques used to gather data or to analyse them.

Methodology: In research, refers to the set of principles and conventions which set out how research should be done and what it can achieve and therefore guides research planning.

Normative: Taking a committed stance about preferred present or future situations.

Ontology: Theory of the nature of 'reality', for example realist or social constructionist.

Operationalisation: The process of defining the elements of a concept in order to make its characteristics more capable of being researched or measured.

Prescriptive: Giving directions about what to do.

Policy trajectory study: A research project which follows a particular policy area from its inception through the various phases of implementation and finally collects data on the outcomes it has brought about, if any.

Realism: An ontological position which posits that an object reality exists which can be apprehended through research.

'So what?' question: The question which runs: "So what is the wider significance of this research to the academic community generally and/or to the economy, society or culture?"

Truth claims: In this context this refers to the claims made for the outcomes of the research in terms of how and where they can be applied and how robust they are.

References

(All websites last accessed 29.7.2014)

Arum, A. And Roksa, J. (2011) *Academically Adrift: Limited learning on college campuses.* Chicago: University of Chicago Press.

Astin, A. (2011) In 'Academically Adrift,' Data Don't Back Up Sweeping Claim. *The Chronicle of Higher Education*, February 14. Available at: http://chronicle.com/article/Academically-Adrift-a/126371/

Ball, S. J. (1995) Intellectuals or Technicians? The urgent role of theory in educational studies. *British Journal of Educational Studies*, 43, 255-271.

Bell, J. *Doing Your Research Project.* London: Open University Press.

Bensimon, E. M., Polkinghorne, D.E., Bauman, G. & Vallejo, E. (2004). Doing Research that Makes a Difference. *The Journal of Higher Education*, 75, 1, 104-126.

Coghlan, D and Brannick, T. (2010) *Doing Action Research in Your Own Organization.* (3rd edition). London: Sage.

Coleman, S. and von Hellermann, P. (2011) *Multi-Sited Ethnography: Problems and possibilities in the translocation of research methods.* London: Routledge.

Cooperrider, D. L. and Srivastva, S. *(1987)* Appreciative Inquiry in Organizational Life. *Research in Organizational Change and Development*, 1, 129-169. Available at http://www.margiehartley.com/home/wp-content/uploads/file/APPRECIATIVE_INQUIRY_IN_Orgnizational_life.pdf

Devault, M. L. (2006) What is Institutional Ethnography? *Social Problems*, 53, 3, 294-298.

Hammersley, M. (1993) On The Teacher As Researcher. In M. Hammersley (ed) *Educational Research: Current issues*. Buckingham: Open University Press.

Haraway, D. J. (1991) *Simians, Cyborgs and Women: The reinvention of nature*. New York: Routledge.

Hey, V. (2006) The Politics Of Performative Resignification: Translating Judith Butler's theoretical discourse and its potential for a sociology of education, *British Journal of Sociology of Education*, 27, 4, 439-457.

Koshy, V. (2009) *Action Research for Improving Educational Practice: A step-by-step guide*. London: Sage (second edition).

Mand, K. (2011) Researching Lives in Motion: Multi-Sited strategies in a transnational context. In S. Coleman and P. von Hellermann (2011) *Multi-Sited Ethnography: Problems and possibilities in the translocation of research methods*. London: Routledge.

Marcus, G. E. (2011) Multi-Sited Ethnography: Five or six things i know about it now. In S. Coleman and P. von Hellermann (2011) *Multi-Sited Ethnography: Problems and possibilities in the translocation of research methods*. London: Routledge.

Patton, Q. M. (1997) *Utilization-Focused Evaluation*. London: Sage. (Third edition).

Pawson, R. and Tilley, N. (1997) *Realistic Evaluation*. London: Sage.

Porter, S. (1993) Critical Realist Ethnography: The case of racism and professionalism in a medical setting. *Sociology*, 7, 4, 591-609.

Saunders, M., Trowler, P. and Bamber, V. (eds) (2011) *Reconceptualising Evaluation in Higher Education: The practice turn*. London: Open University Press.

Smith, D. E. (2005) *Institutional Ethnography: A sociology for people*. Lanham, MD: AltaMira.

Sprague, J. and Hayes, J. (2000) Self-Determination and Empowerment: A feminist standpoint analysis of talk about disability. *American Journal of Community Psychology*, 28, 5, 671-695.

Trowler, P. (2001) Captured By The Discourse? the socially constitutive power of new higher education discourse in the UK. *Organization*, 8, 2, 183-201.

Trowler, P. (2012) Wicked Issues in Situating Theory in Close Up Research. *Higher Education Research and Development*. 31, 3, 273-284.

****

All Rights Reserved © 2014 Paul Trowler

Printed in Great Britain
by Amazon.co.uk, Ltd.,
Marston Gate.